The Joy of Parenthood

Inspiration and Encouragement for Parents

by Jan Blaustone

 Meadowbrook Press

Distributed by Simon & Schuster
New York

Distributed in the U.K. by
Chris Lloyd Sales and Marketing

Library of Congress Cataloging-in-Publication Data

Blaustone, Jan.
    Joy of parenthood: inspiration and encouragement for parents / by Jan Blaustone.
        p. cm.
    1. Parenthood—Miscellanea.   2. Parent and child—Miscellanea.   I. Title
HQ755.8.B6   1993
306.874—dc20   92-40271
                                                                            CIP

ISBN 0-88166-198-8

Simon & Schuster Ordering # 0-671-86778-4

Editor: Bruce Lansky
Editorial Coordinator: Elizabeth Weiss
Desktop Publishing Coordinator: Jon C. Wright
Production Coordinator: Matthew Thurber
Designer: Tabor Harlow
Cover Art: Erik Broberg

Published by Meadowbrook Press, 5451 Smetana Drive, Minnetonka, MN 55343.

BOOK TRADE DISTRIBUTION by Simon & Schuster, a division of Simon and Schuster, Inc.,
1230 Avenue of the Americas, New York, NY 10020.

First published in the U.K. 1993.
DISTRIBUTED IN THE U.K. AND IRELAND by Chris Lloyd Sales and Marketing,
P.O. Box 327, Poole, Dorset BH15 2RG.

98 97   10 9 8 7 6

Printed in the United States of America

Acknowledgments

There never seems to be the right time or place to thank my husband, Michael, and in my haste I often fail to mention my gratitude to him. Everyone should be so fortunate to have a mate who faithfully picks them up when they are down and enables them to touch the sky. Michael, for the countless times I have failed to thank you, let me thank you now.

The author also gratefully acknowledges the exceptional work done by the photographers who contributed real shots of families doing what comes naturally.

Photographs: p. viii by Cassie Bunker; pp. 37 and 74 by Pam Demonbreun; p. 41 by Mary Entrekin; p. 98 by Michael Hughs; p. 20 by Dan Keeslar; p. 55 by Rick Lance; pp. 90 and 103 by Les Leverett; pp. 62, 66, 71, 82, 87, and 95 by Libby Leverett-Crew; pp. 10 and 25 by Nancy Libby; p. 45 by Steve Lowry; p. 50 by Sherry McManus; p. 79 by Anna Doreen Serb; and p. 17 by Ross Smith.

Dedication

This little book is dedicated to our son, Lee Michael Blaustone, who not only inspired the book, but continues to inspire us every day.

Good things come in small packages, and they take a long time to get here. Little Lee, we have no idea why we were chosen to be your parents, but we're forever thankful.

Each day that we know you, we admire you a little bit more. We hope we are half the inspiration to you as you are to us.

With love,
Mama

Preface

We are all caretakers of the children.
They're on loan to us for a limited time,
and only the loaner knows for how long.

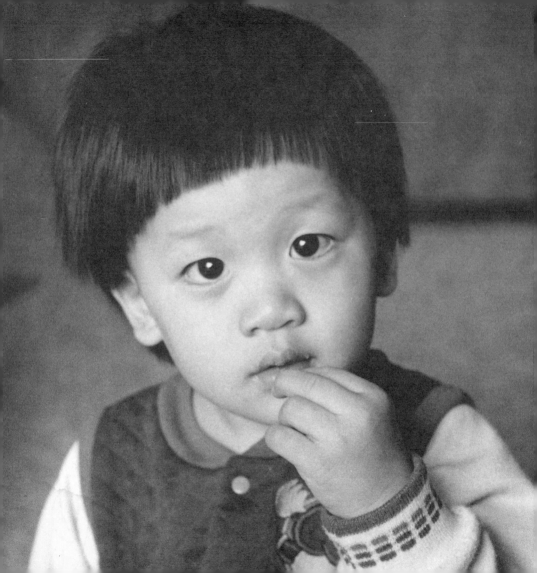

Introduction

Children are life's most precious resource. They determine our future. They carry on family legacies. They inspire our everyday lives and provide us with an opportunity to make a difference. While there is no greater responsibility than being a parent, there is no greater reward than raising children.

I knew all this years ago. But I didn't understand it until June 18, 1986. After five years of marriage, we threw out the old argument that we couldn't afford kids, and I became pregnant. But we never heard our child's heartbeat. I miscarried four days after my thirty-first birthday. Six months later I was diagnosed with muscular dystrophy, a neurological disorder thought to be genetic. I chose to become sterile, and we prayed for an adoption.

Four years passed until one cold January morning when our social worker from the Tennessee Department of Human Services presented us with our five pound, six-week-old son. We bundled him up in disbelief and drove home, never taking our eyes off him.

This little book is a tribute to all our son has taught us in his first two years of life. It's a book of encouragement for every parent—about hanging on in spite of the odds and creating your own light when only darkness surrounds you. If you haven't any children, love a child who hasn't any parents. Although adoption wasn't part of our plan, now we can't imagine our life any other way.

To many, this book will bring back memories of precious days that slipped away all too soon. To others, I hope it serves as a reminder to persist in seeking what you want out of life. Believe in your abilities, and when it's your turn, become the best parent you can possibly be. Take the job seriously, and you'll be rewarded in more ways than you ever dreamed possible.

John Blaustone

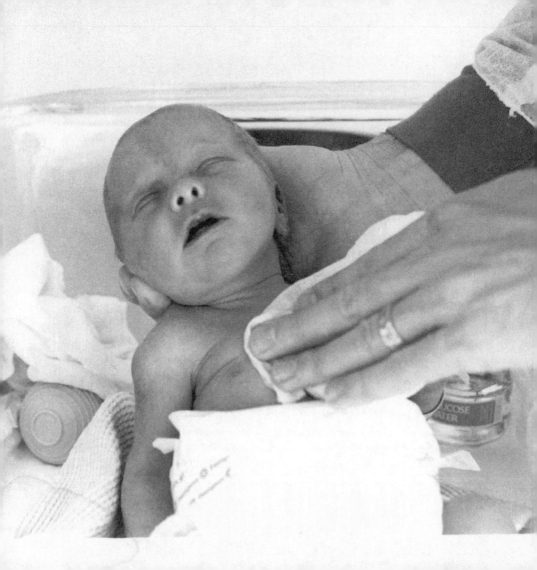

A miracle happens every day when a child is born.

When you want a child, you have a lot to hope for. When you have a child, you have a lot to live for.

Parenthood isn't like fishing—every child is a keeper.

Parents are gamblers, risking their hearts to pain for a potential jackpot of joy.

It's hard to explain the joy that parenthood can add to your life—especially to people who don't have children. They just look at you and smile, thinking you've gone bananas.

Looking at your baby asleep in your arms gives you unimaginable joy. You wonder how you lived so long without her.

Every baby is a gift from above wrapped in a ribbon of joy.

Leave it to a baby to turn your world upside down, take your breath away, and make you fall in love again. With his toothless grin, your baby sets your heart on fire.

Sometimes you think you can barely take care of yourself, and yet here you are holding your new baby. Someone up there must believe in you.

Courage and faith in your abilities make a great beginning for parenthood—all you add is love.

Parents of every nation want their children
to live in a world where they can grow up
safe from harm, free from oppression,
and proud of their heritage. In this
way, we're all alike.

To love and be loved is every child's birthright.

Children are born color blind, loving all people.

Every mothers' eyes tell a story of hope, strength, and pride—no matter what their color.

The biggest surprise in parenthood is that hanging out with your baby is fun.

While you can't recall what you did with your newborn all day, somehow it took every minute of your time.

Newborn twins go through eighteen diapers a day. Don't you feel better already?

Moms should tell dads just how good they look with a diaper bag over their shoulder.

Some things will never change:

1. Baby cribs never come with all their parts.

2. Leak-proof diapers aren't.

3. Everyone else's newborn sleeps through the night.

Colic is probably the surest method of birth control.

Leaning against your legs, she plays quietly at your feet. Without talking, she lets you know she's happy. It feels good just to have her there.

Down he falls again. "Pick yourself up, little one," you say, "because you have a thousand more to go."

Give your little one a grape juice popsicle. Watch him smear it all over his face and hair. It drips a lot, staining his clothes. He waves it furiously, barely hanging on to the end of the stick. He puts the wrong end in his mouth. It drips some more. Finally, he flings it across the room. It smacks into the wall, leaving a purple stain, and falls to the floor in a puddle. As you attempt to wash his face, check yourself. Are you still smiling?

When you talk to your child, have a real nose-to-nose dialogue. Get down on her level so you can see what she sees and feel what she feels.

Morning routines with a toddler are anything but routine.

Toys are magnetically attracted to the bottom of parents' feet.

Getting your toddler into the tub can be as hard as getting him out.

Toddlers are more likely to eat healthy food if they find it on the floor.

The secret to feeding your child is learning how to disguise a vegetable as a french fry.

Nothing puts a smile on your face faster than a two-year-old eating spaghetti.

Think of the "terrible twos" as a dress rehearsal for the adolescent years.

Love will not last unless it is nurtured; children will not thrive unless they are loved.

You can't help but love your kids—even when they almost drive you nuts.

Don't tell your two-year-old she's driving you nuts. She just might say, "Mama nuts," to everyone she meets.

Children push your buttons to see how you'll react—that's how they learn.

Parenthood teaches you to roll with the punches.

The best thing to save for a rainy day is your patience.

Children with special needs present their parents
with special gifts.

Every child is gifted—it is the parents' job to help
their children express their talent.

All children are capable of shining when given
the opportunity.

All parents want their children to have
opportunities that they never had.

Before you try to give your children what you
didn't have, give them what you do have.

The two most valuable things you can give your
child are your time and attention.

Your children are your greatest gifts in life.
Caring for them well is your "thank you."

There are no magic answers when it comes to
raising children—but there are many magic
moments.

When making choices for your child, think back
to your own childhood and what made you happy.

Make time to play with your child *today.*

Parents experience the sweet and simple pleasures in life that matter most of all.

Life with a child is like reading a good mystery. It's the element of surprise that makes both so wonderful.

A child with an imagination is never lonely.

A happy childhood is built to last.

It's hard to be a grown-up when you're among children—it's like walking by a grand piano without playing a few notes.

Although you may not always have the energy to play ball, you'll always be glad you did.

You can always tell the age of someone's kids by how high up the good china sits on the shelf.

Only you can appreciate every little thing your child makes. Up it goes on the refrigerator door— even if you're not quite sure what it is.

Although your child means the world to you, he's just a kid to everyone else.

Learning to be a good parent begins during childhood.

Parenthood is a little like basketball. It feels great to pass the ball and watch your child score.

Parents all over the world "go for the gold" every day by trying to be the best parents possible.

Be generous with your child's needs and conservative with her wants. More importantly, know the difference.

No matter how few toys a child might have, he is only deprived if he is unloved.

The more love your family shares, the less "stuff" your family needs.

Love and acceptance are what every child needs
and what every parent can afford to give.

Children need roots and wings.

It is impossible for a child to have too much
self-esteem.

Give your child the courage to follow
her dreams.

By believing in possibilities, you'll naturally
encourage your child to do the same.

The things that make kids different are the very
things that make them special.

The most common characteristic in children is
that every child is unique.

Believe Grandma when she says, "Honey, it's just
trial and error. Every kid is different."

Kids are as unpredictable as an August thunderstorm—but summer is still a favorite time of year.

Your child is like Mom's homemade cookies—no one else's can compare.

Once you have a second child, you realize that having the first one didn't make you an expert.

Children should be both seen *and* heard.

Some of life's greatest truths are voiced by children.

Feed your child's mind as well as his body.

Read twice as many children's books as
parenting manuals.

Reading a story to your child every night is as
good for you as it is for her.

No matter how big you become, you're never too big to be small again.

The way to keep your imagination alive is to use it. The way to keep your dreams alive is to live them. Let your children show you how.

A child will show you courage when all you feel is fear. A child will give you hope when all you know is despair.

The more you learn from your children, the more you realize just how much they can teach you.

Learn from your children what you forgot along the road to adulthood.

Everyone is a child at heart, but sometimes it takes a child to remind us.

The day you no longer want to play with your children is the day you are "old."

A little kid and a big dog hanging their heads out the window of a station wagon with their noses to the wind know something about life that most grown-ups forget somewhere along the way.

Snow days are life's reminder to have fun. Go sledding with your kids and drink some hot chocolate with tiny marshmallows. *Then* worry about shoveling the driveway.

When you forget how to smile, watch your child at play.

Be comfortable with uncertainty. Instead of trying to predict the future, enjoy each moment.

You can't read your child's mind, but you can guess what's in her heart.

We could all use a dose of mothering now and then.

Hear your child's song, share his mood, catch his rhythm—stay in tune.

Your children don't care how much you know. They care how much you care.

The greatest handicap of all is an inability to love.

Hold your child's hand now, while you still can.

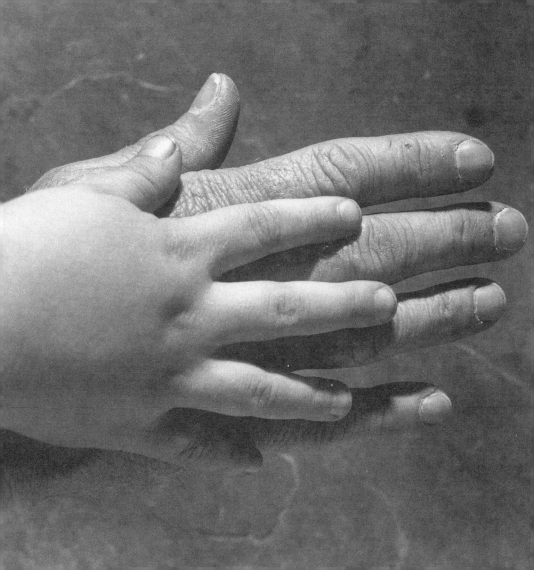

Every once in a while, a mother will notice that she's sounding an awful lot like her own mother.

Remember all the times when your mother called you by your sister's name? Don't be surprised to find yourself doing the same thing.

When you want to be heard, never begin a sentence with, "How many times have I told you. . . ."

Parenthood teaches you that there is more than one answer to every question in life.

You never really know what working overtime is until you become a parent.

It's not the load that weighs you down—it's how you carry it.

For an immediate response from your children, relax on the couch with your feet up. It draws attention like a bullhorn.

You can't have a clean house with kids around any more than you can have a clean car after driving through a mud puddle.

It's part of the "kids' credo" to always prefer someone else's lunch to the one Mom made.

With children come new stains on the carpet,
new dents in the coffee table, and new joys
in your life.

Family life can be messy, but you can't plant a
garden without getting in the dirt.

Never hand your child the garden hose unless
you're near the faucet.

Nobody makes all the right decisions. Take comfort in knowing you're doing your very best. Having done your best, you'll have nothing to regret.

The more love you give your children, the more they overlook your shortcomings.

Your children may forget what you say, but they never forget how you make them feel.

It is as rewarding to watch your child imitate your best traits as it is painful to watch her imitate your worst.

Parents don't deserve blame for all their children's shortcomings any more than they deserve praise for all their children's accomplishments.

Smile! A little humor goes a long way.

One of life's greatest joys is to see smiles on your children's faces and sparkles in their eyes.

Children's smiles translate into every language.

Before we can make peace with our neighbors,
we must first make peace within our families.

Kindness is contagious. Pass it on.

You can run out of many things, but never run
out of hugs and kisses.

When you need a lift, lift your child up and
hug him.

When your child hurts, you hurt.
Comfort each other.

You don't fully appreciate the healing power of
love until the day your child kisses your hurt
away and tells you that everything will be
all right.

The world needs more hugging. That's what the arms race should be about.

What a child learns today determines his
character tomorrow.

What you learn in life has great value. Sharing it
with your child gives you great pleasure.

Learn by observing. Communicate by listening.
Teach by example.

Children follow in your footsteps faster than they follow your advice.

Your child will see through you. Give her something to look at.

If you want an honest child, be an honest parent.

Time spent with your family doing ordinary things is the most extraordinary time of all.

Of all your worldly possessions, your family is the most valuable.

Your children are always a better measure of your success than your bank account.

The best way to secure your future is to invest time in your children.

The real bonuses in life are given by your children—not your employer.

Jobs may come and go, but families are forever.

Becoming your child's best friend is the greatest bonus of all.

If only there were a way to make all the
precious moments last.

You can never have too many photographs
of your children.

Not too long ago, you used to tuck her under your arm like a football. Now she's become her own little person. You just never thought the time would come so soon.

No matter how many years go by, he'll always be your little pumpkin, and you'll always be his biggest hero.

Kids used to bicycle to the park in torn jeans to play ball with whoever happened to show up. They didn't have uniforms, organized leagues, official rules, coaches, or bleachers full of cheering parents—but they sure did have fun.

The purpose of play is to have fun—it's a rule parents sometimes forget in the heat of competition.

Kids grow up so quickly. Smudges on the sliding glass door get higher and higher, until one day you look, and they're gone. All that remain are the memories.

Spend time with your kids. Don't analyze it.
Don't criticize it. Just do it.

When your children recall their childhood,
let them say, "Those were the good
old days."

You know your child is growing up when he realizes that you won't "fix" every mess he gets into.

Kids ask questions until puberty. Then they know all the answers, and the parents ask all the questions.

No matter how big your children grow, they never outgrow their need for affection.

Hugs are more reassuring than words.

The best medicine in the world isn't as strong as a mother's kiss.

A young girl may dream of becoming a princess, but in the eyes of her parents, she already is.

Being both a good parent *and* a good spouse is a monumental achievement.

The best "security blanket" a child can have is parents who respect each other.

A single parent with conviction is more powerful than two who disagree.

While marriage isn't always "till death do us part," parenthood truly is.

A family is made up of people who love one another.

Give your child a crash course in love and attention. Repeat the course every day of every year.

"Quality time" begins with your marriage. What's good for your marriage is good for your children.

Listen to your parents. Life is a little easier when you learn from people who have lived more of it.

The best way to repay your parents is to give your children all the love your own parents gave you—and then some.

You're never too old to dance in the kitchen or kiss for no reason.

The prettiest "girls" in the world are your wife at fifty, your mother at seventy, and your daughter at birth.

It is a proud moment when your grandchild entrusts you with his secrets.

Unconditional love is the best legacy.

The joy of raising your family far outweighs the heartache of watching them leave.

Your daughter may leave home, but she'll never leave your heart.

There's no greater thrill than the birth of your first child until the birth of your first grandchild.

When you have a grandchild, you always have something to talk about.

Grandparents enjoy spoiling their grandchildren almost as much as their grandchildren enjoy being spoiled.

Believe your parents when they say,
"The best is yet to come."

One of the greatest joys of being a grandparent is rediscovering the wonder of life through the eyes of your grandchild.

Your favorite childhood games are even more fun when you play them with your grandchildren.

Keep lots of family albums—leave a paper trail for your grandchildren to follow.

Raising a family changes people—it makes them better.

Now that you finally realize all the things
your parents did for you, thank them.

Order Form

Qty.	Title	Author	Order #	Unit Cost	Total
	Baby & Child Emergency First Aid	Einzig, M.	1380	$15.00	
	Baby & Child Medical Care	Hart, T	1159	$9.00	
	Baby Journal	Bennett, M.	3172	$10.00	
	Baby Name Personality Survey	Lansky/Sinrod	1270	$8.00	
	Best Baby Shower Book	Cooke, C.	1239	$7.00	
	Child Care A to Z	Woolfson	1010	$11.00	
	Dads Say the Dumbest Things!	Lansky/Jones	4220	$6.00	
	Familiarity Breeds Children	Lansky, B.	4015	$7.00	
	Feed Me! I'm Yours	Lansky, V.	1109	$9.00	
	First-Year Baby Care	Kelly, P.	1119	$9.00	
	Getting Organized for Your Baby	Bard, M.	1229	$9.00	
	Grandma Knows Best	McBride, M.	4009	$7.00	
	How to Pamper Your Pregnant Wife	Schultz/Schultz	1140	$7.00	
	Joy of Parenthood	Blaustone, J.	3500	$7.00	
	Maternal Journal	Bennett, M.	3171	$10.00	
	Moms Say the Funniest Things!	Lansky, B.	4280	$6.00	
	Practical Parenting Tips	Lansky, V.	1180	$8.00	
	Very Best Baby Name Book	Lansky, B.	1030	$8.00	
				Subtotal	
		Shipping and Handling (see below)			
		MN residents add 6.5% sales tax			
				Total	

YES! Please send me the books indicated above. Add $2.00 shipping and handling for the first book and 50¢ for each additional book. Add $2.50 to total for books shipped to Canada. Overseas postage will be billed. Allow up to four weeks for delivery. Send check or money order payable to Meadowbrook Press. No cash or COD's, please. Prices subject to change without notice. **Quantity discounts available upon request.**

Send book(s) to:

Name _____ Address _____

City _____ State ___ Zip _____ Telephone (_____) _____

P.O. number (if necessary) _____ **Payment via:** ❏ Check or money order payable to Meadowbrook Press

Amount enclosed $ _____ ❏ Visa ❏ MasterCard (for orders over $10.00 only)

Account # _____ Signature _____ Exp. Date _____

A *FREE* Meadowbrook Press catalog is available upon request.

Mail to: Meadowbrook Press
5451 Smetana Drive, Minnetonka, MN 55343

Phone (612) 930-1100   Toll-Free 1-800-338-2232   Fax (612) 930-1940